disc

My Path to Math

PROBABILITY

Marina Cohen

Crabtree Publishing Company

www.crabtreebooks.com

Author: Marina Cohen
Publishing plan research and development:
  Sean Charlebois, Reagan Miller
  Crabtree Publishing Company
Editor: Molly Aloian
Editorial director: Kathy Middleton
Project coordinator: Margaret Salter
Prepress technician: Margaret Salter
Coordinating editor: Chester Fisher
Series editor: Jessica Cohn
Project manager: Kumar Kunal (Q2AMEDIA)
Art direction: Rahul Dhiman (Q2AMEDIA)
Cover design: Shruti Aggarwal (Q2AMEDIA)
Design: Shruti Aggarwal (Q2AMEDIA)
Photo research: Ekta Sharma (Q2AMEDIA)

Photographs:
Shutterstock: Vladimir Wrangel: p. 4; Ppart. p. 8;
  South12th Photography: p. 19 (top)
Ray Barlow: front cover, title page, p. 5, p. 7, p. 9, p. 11,
  p. 15, p. 16, p. 17 (top and bottom), p. 21, p. 23
Fotolia: Cory Thoman: p. 7 (top)
Istockphoto: Brian McEntire: p. 19 (bottom)
Q2AMedia Art Bank: p. 13, p. 15

Library and Archives Canada Cataloguing in Publication

Cohen, Marina
    Probability / Marina Cohen.

(My path to math)
Includes index.
ISBN 978-0-7787-5249-3 (bound).--ISBN 978-0-7787-5296-7 (pbk.)

    1. Probabilities--Juvenile literature. I. Title. II. Series: My path
to math

QA273.16.C63 2009   j519.2   C2009-905365-9

Library of Congress Cataloging-in-Publication Data

Cohen, Marina.
  Probability / Marina Cohen.
    p. cm. -- (My path to math)
  Includes index.

  ISBN 978-0-7787-5296-7 (pbk. : alk. paper) -- ISBN 978-0-7787-5249-3 (reinforced
library binding : alk. paper)
  1. Probabilities--Juvenile literature. I. Title. II. Series.

  QA273.16.C64 2010
  519.2--dc22

                                                    2009035497

Crabtree Publishing Company

www.crabtreebooks.com   1-800-387-7650

Printed in China/122009/CT20090903

Published in Canada
Crabtree Publishing
616 Welland Ave.
St. Catharines, ON
L2M 5V6

Published in the United States
Crabtree Publishing
PMB 59051
350 Fifth Avenue, 59th Floor
New York, New York 10118

Published in the United Kingdom
Crabtree Publishing
Maritime House
Basin Road North, Hove
BN41 1WR

Published in Australia
Crabtree Publishing
386 Mt. Alexander Rd.
Ascot Vale (Melbourne)
VIC 3032

Contents

Flip a Coin

It is raining. Ella can invite James or Alex over. She flips a coin to decide which friend to call. If the coin lands on heads, she will invite James. If it lands on tails, she will invite Alex.

Each friend has a 1 in 2 **chance** of being invited. Each friend has an **equal** chance.

Activity Box

Flip a coin 20 times. Write down what happens on a chart like this one. What do you notice?

heads	✓			✓	✓		✓	✓
tails		✓	✓			✓		

Ella flips a coin. Will the coin show heads or tails?

Impossible!

Tails! Ella calls Alex to see if he can visit. She also asks if his sister will let them borrow her video games. Alex says that will happen when pigs fly.

Ella laughs. She knows that pigs cannot fly. That is impossible! That means there is zero chance of getting the games. That **event** will never happen.

Activity Box

Complete the following chart. Write one or two more events under each heading.

always	more likely	less likely	never
You will be older on your next birthday.	You will smile at least once today.	You will travel to another country tonight.	You will grow a second head.

What chance is there that pigs will fly?

On a Roll

Ella and Alex select a board game. The players must roll a number cube. The cube has six sides. Each side has a number of dots, from 1 to 6.

To begin the game, they must each roll the cube. The person with the highest number goes first. Ella knows she has a 1 in 6 chance of rolling a 6. Rolling a 6 is one of six possible **outcomes**.

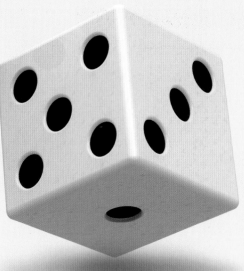

Activity Box

On a chart like this, show the six possible outcomes using dots and the number of dots.

• 1					

Ella wants to roll a 6.

Keep Rolling

Ella does not roll a 6 with her first roll. She does not roll a 6 in any of the six rolls that she gets. Why not?

A number cube does not roll out the numbers from 1 to 6 in order. Each roll is a brand-new turn. It is an **independent** event. Ella has one chance of rolling a 6. She has five chances of not rolling 6. It is more likely that she will not roll a 6.

Roll 1	Roll 2
6	6
5	5
④	4
3	3
2	②
1	1

◀ Ella rolls a 4 the first time. She rolls a 2 the second time.

Ella has a big number cube, too.
The dots are the same, from 1 to 6!

Give It a Spin

The two friends then play a game with a spinner. The spinner has three equal sections. One section is blue. Another section is red. The third section is yellow.

Players have a 1 in 3 chance of landing on blue. Ella and Alex take turns spinning the spinner. They **record** the results.

Activity Box

Trace and cut out a circle on paper. Divide it into three equal spaces. Color one space red, one blue, and one yellow. Put the point of a pencil through a paperclip. Point the pencil to the spot where the colors meet. Spin the clip around the pencil and see what color it stops on. Spin it 15 times. Record the results.

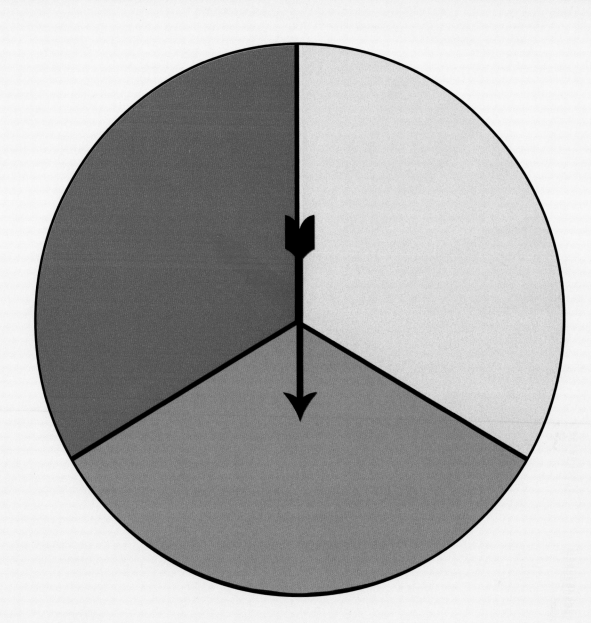

Name	Red	Blue	Yellow
Ella		✓	
Alex			

The chances of landing on each color are one in three.

Take Another Spin

The spinner breaks! Alex suggests that they make a new one. They draw a circle and try to color it like their first spinner. But their spaces are **uneven**. This means the chances of landing on a color will no longer be even.

Activity Box

Create a spinner with three uneven spaces. Color the smallest space red, the medium space blue, and the largest space yellow. Stand a pencil at the center, with the point inside a paper clip. Spin the clip around the point 15 times. Record your results each time. How are the results different this time?

The plastic arrow in the center breaks off! Now what?

Not Fair!

Ella is tired of playing games.
She wants to make up a dance.
Alex wants to read books instead.
They flip a coin to decide.

"Heads, I win. Tails, you lose!"
says Alex.

"Not fair," says Ella. "It is **certain**
you will win!"

Ella cannot win. She is not
laughing at Alex's joke!

◀ Heads! I win!

◀ Tails! You lose!

Snack Time

"We need a snack," says Ella. She puts a small bowl on the table. It has three carrot sticks and four celery sticks. She tells Alex to reach in without looking and see what he gets. He **predicts** it will be celery. Why? There are more celery sticks than carrots. The chances of pulling a celery stick from the bowl are better.

The carrots and celery sticks make seven snacks altogether. There are four celery sticks. So there is a 4 in 7 chance he will pick celery.

Activity Box

Mark a black dot on three pennies. Then place the three marked pennies and six unmarked pennies in a bag. Reach in. Predict whether you will pull out a penny with a dot. Are you right? Try adding unmarked pennies. Or try subtracting unmarked pennies.

Alex knows there are more
celery sticks than carrots.

See You Soon

Ella and Alex have had a fun day. They learned about **probability** by playing games. Probability is a measure of how likely something is.

Ella and Alex learned about chances by rolling a number cube. They learned more about chances when using a spinner. They found out that spinners with even and uneven sections give players different chances.

"I liked playing board games today," says Ella.

"I always like the snacks!" says Alex.

They both laugh.

You can use the glossary and index on the pages that follow to look back at the math ideas in the book.

Glossary

certain Sure to happen

chance Something that happens that cannot be guessed correctly ahead of time.

equal Matching in number or size

event Thing that happens at a certain time and in a certain place

independent Happens separately from something else and has no effect on that thing

outcomes When playing games, the results of the moves and choices a player makes

predicts Guesses ahead of time based on how likely certain outcomes are

probability Measure of how likely something is

record To mark the results so they can be studied

uneven Not matching in number or size

Index